# CELEBRATING THE FAMILY NAME OF LEWIS

# Celebrating the Family Name of Lewis

## Walter the Educator

Silent King Books
a WhichHead Entertainment Imprint

Copyright © 2024 by Walter the Educator

All rights reserved. No part of this book may be reproduced in any manner whatsoever without written permission except in the case of brief quotations embodied in critical articles and reviews.

First Printing, 2024

Disclaimer

This book is a literary work; the story is not about specific persons, locations, situations, and/or circumstances unless mentioned in a historical context. Any resemblance to real persons, locations, situations, and/or circumstances is coincidental. This book is for entertainment and informational purposes only. The author and publisher offer this information without warranties expressed or implied. No matter the grounds, neither the author nor the publisher will be accountable for any losses, injuries, or other damages caused by the reader's use of this book. The use of this book acknowledges an understanding and acceptance of this disclaimer.

Celebrating the Family Name of Lewis is a memory book that belongs to the Celebrating Family Name Book Series by Walter the Educator. Collect them all and more books at WaltertheEducator.com

**USE THE EXTRA SPACE TO DOCUMENT YOUR FAMILY MEMORIES THROUGHOUT THE YEARS**

# LEWIS

In the early morning's golden light,

Celebrating the Family Name of

# Lewis

Where dawn breaks free from the clutch of night,

The name of Lewis takes its place,

A legacy of strength and grace.

From rolling hills to ocean's edge,

Where winds of change make their pledge,

The Lewis name stands firm and true,

A beacon bright in every view.

Through ages past, in lands of green,

Where rivers flow and forests teem,

The Lewis family found their way,

A story written every day.

With hands that build, with minds that dream,

The Lewis name is like a stream,

Flowing strong, with endless might,

Carving paths through day and night.
Celebrating the Family Name of

# Lewis

Their roots run deep in history's soil,

With hearts that beat, with endless toil,

The name of Lewis echoes clear,

A melody that all can hear.

In every dawn, in every dusk,

The Lewis name, a trusted husk,

Protecting seeds of hope and love,

A gift from those who dwell above.

Through trials faced and battles fought,

The Lewis name has never sought,

To turn away, to hide, to fear,

For in their hearts, they hold it dear.

The laughter of their children plays,

In fields where golden sunlight stays,

A testament to life and joy,

Celebrating the Family Name of

# Lewis

For every Lewis girl and boy.

In every challenge, every test,

The Lewis spirit does its best,

To rise above, to stand its ground,

In every heart, their strength is found.

Through winter's cold and summer's heat,

The Lewis name will not retreat,

With courage bold, with eyes of fire,

## Celebrating the Family Name of

# Lewis

They climb the peaks, they rise, aspire.

# ABOUT THE CREATOR

Walter the Educator is one of the pseudonyms for Walter Anderson. Formally educated in Chemistry, Business, and Education, he is an educator, an author, a diverse entrepreneur, and he is the son of a disabled war veteran. "Walter the Educator" shares his time between educating and creating. He holds interests and owns several creative projects that entertain, enlighten, enhance, and educate, hoping to inspire and motivate you. Follow, find new works, and stay up to date with Walter the Educator™

**at WaltertheEducator.com**

www.ingramcontent.com/pod-product-compliance
Lightning Source LLC
LaVergne TN
LVHW010622070526
838199LV00063BA/5234